Original title:
Craters of Creativity

Copyright © 2025 Creative Arts Management OÜ
All rights reserved.

Author: Riley Donovan
ISBN HARDBACK: 978-1-80567-823-6
ISBN PAPERBACK: 978-1-80567-944-8

Wellsprings of Ingenuity

In a land where ideas collide,
Balloons burst and giggles abide.
Outlandish thoughts, an amusing race,
With each wild plan, we find our place.

Socks become puppets, hats take flight,
Doodles dance in the pale moonlight.
A mishap leads to laughter's spark,
When ideas bloom in the deep, dark park.

Jellybeans sing when no one's near,
While jigsaw pieces whisper, "Hey, cheer!"
Every blunder forms a new delight,
As quirks and flukes take center stage tonight.

A teapot spins tales of time gone past,
A paper crane dreams, soaring fast.
In this playground where thoughts can roam,
We craft our laughter, we build our home.

Echoes of Imagination's Depths

In a land where thoughts collide,
Doodles dance and giggles hide.
Ideas bubble, then they burst,
In the chaos, laughter's first.

Rubber chickens float on air,
Puns can grow like weeds with flair.
A thinking cap that's far too tight,
Adds to the silliness of night.

Whispers from the Well of Invention

Down the well, there's much to hear,
Silly gadgets hold us near.
A spoon that sings, a hat that squeaks,
Innovation plays hide and seeks.

Tickle the ivories, or so they say,
When rubber ducks demand to play.
Ideas bounce, then fall like rain,
Fill the puddles, giggle in vain.

The Canvas of Cosmic Thought

On a canvas of stars and dreams,
Scribbles dance in cosmic beams.
There's a rocket made of candy canes,
And aliens with funny names.

Crayons fly and paint the scene,
Mountains made of whipped cream.
Brushes chat and giggle too,
Creating worlds, all askew.

Shadows Cast by Innovation's Light

In shadows where ideas loom,
Monsters march with broomstick brooms.
Twisted thoughts that come alive,
Make a circus where we thrive.

Pens that roll and pencils talk,
Crazy creatures take a walk.
Join the parade of loony sights,
Underneath the wacky lights.

Secrets of the Well

In a well where ideas dive,
A rubber duck will arrive.
With a splash, the thoughts take flight,
Making bubbles of pure delight.

Secrets swirl in shades of blue,
Each one giggles, laughs, and coos.
A grumpy frog starts to croak,
Wishing for a talking joke.

Down below, the fish take bets,
On how long the laughter gets.
The well is deep, but never sad,
With an echo of the wacky mad.

So bring your whims and toss a stone,
Listen close to thoughts unknown.
In this well of giggles, find,
A treasure trove for playful minds.

Vortexes of Vision

In a whirlpool of wild sight,
Monkeys dance with sheer delight.
They toss ideas like confetti,
While a parrot spins, oh so petty.

A twist and turn, a dizzy flight,
Silly hats that fit too tight.
Visions blend in taffy hue,
Juicy thoughts, like morning dew.

Around the swirl, the laughter flows,
Tickling toes, and bumping nose.
The vortex giggles, spins anew,
Chasing dreams, and eating stew.

Jump on in, let swirling start,
Join the fun, ignite your heart.
For in this storm of silly play,
You'll find the bright, creative way.

Gates to the Abstract

Oh, the gates of colors bright,
Swing wide open, what a sight!
A cat in glasses reads a book,
While turtles dance, and zebras cook.

Shapes and swirls in crazy streams,
Make you giggle at your dreams.
A spiral stairs leads to the moon,
With raccoons playing a jazzy tune.

Through the gates, a feast awaits,
Of wobbly chairs and laughing plates.
A broken clock ticks out of tune,
While juggling fish will make you swoon.

So step right through and join the jest,
Where nonsense reigns and dreams are blessed.
In this world of whacky tones,
Creativity, as wild as moans.

Journeys Through the Unknown

On a journey to the place unseen,
Jumping puddles of jelly bean.
With rubber boots and candy canes,
We wander through the silly lanes.

A dragon's sneeze, a bubble burst,
To the land of giggle-first.
Where marshmallow clouds take a rest,
And penguins wear their Sunday best.

Adventure calls, but wait, oh dear!
A pie flies by—oh, have no fear.
We'll ride on llamas, jump so high,
As ice cream falls like confetti sky.

In this land of funny sights,
Join us for our wild flights.
Where dreams are mixed with laughter's song,
And every step just feels so wrong.

Tides of Expression

Waves of laughter crash ashore,
Dancing ideas that want to explore.
A wink from a muse with silly grace,
Each splash is a smile upon your face.

Colors swirl like jellybeans,
Ink spills out in silly scenes.
A giggle turns to a loud guffaw,
Let's sketch a gnome with a cape and paw.

Portals to Possibility

Open a door to a land of vines,
Where socks are hats and cats draw lines.
Jump through the window, what do you find?
Bananas that sing and trees that rhyme.

Twinkle-toed fairies dance on the ground,
They trade silly secrets without making a sound.
Every corner hides a riddle to share,
In a land where crumbs always lead to a bear.

Labyrinth of Ideas

Round and round in a thought-filled maze,
Dodging logic in a playful haze.
A bubblegum tree whispers to me,
To dance with doodles near a bumblebee.

Twisting paths of dreams and schemes,
Where marshmallow clouds float in fluffed-up beams.
Try to catch a thought like a butterfly,
But laugh when it flutters and says goodbye!

Chasms of Curiosity

Peering down into a funny pit,
Where rubber chickens take a seat and sit.
Curious creatures with googly eyes,
Inventing new worlds beneath the skies.

A balance beam made of spaghetti strands,
Where jellyfish juggle in wobbly bands.
Each question tumbles and spins around,
In this twitchy world, joyfully unbound.

Radiance Beyond the Surface

In the land of bright ideas, a shade of whimsy lies,
Where thoughts bounce like bunnies and laughter fills the skies.
Colors blend like jellybeans, splattered all around,
Every giggle, every chuckle, a new joy to be found.

A paintbrush dipped in nonsense, we swirl it with delight,

Like unicorns on pogo sticks, popping in the night.
The canvas comes alive with hopscotch lines of fun,
A masterpiece of humor, dancing 'til we're done.

Strokes of the Bold

With brushes made of marshmallows, we splash the colors bright,
Creating worlds of giggles that shimmer in the light.
Each stroke a silly secret, each drip a playful jest,
We craft our own adventures, putting laughter to the test.

Like penguins in a limbo, we wiggle and we sway,
Twisting through our sketches in a baffling ballet.
Doodling dreams like jellyfish, floating in the air,
Yarn and giggles intertwine, with stories we can share.

Crystals of Thought

Sparkly gems of jesting, they twinkle in the mind,
Shiny bits of nonsense, in laughter we can find.
Each thought a cheeky sparkle, like stars that dance and spin,
With humor as our treasure, we uncover joy within.

In caves of crazy stories, we dig with all our might,
Unearthing jokes and fun times, shimmering so bright.
A chandelier of whimsy, it glimmers on the wall,
Each crystal tells a secret, come on, let's have a ball!

Unearthing Inspiration

In a garden full of giggles, where flowers bloom with glee,
We dig for bright ideas that tiptoe like a bee.
A shovel made of laughter, we scratch beneath the ground,

Finding roots of silly whimsies that twirl and spin around.

With worms in funny hats, we plant our seeds of cheer,
And water them with chuckles, while butterflies all cheer.

Each sprout a new adventure, a path of silly dreams,
Unearthing all the wonders is easier than it seems.

Traces of the Invisible

In the back of the fridge, ideas do dwell,
Moldy and quirky, they ring like a bell.
A sneeze from a cat, oh what a great muse,
Creating a riddle from yesterday's blues.

A sock on the floor, it wiggles about,
Whispers of nonsense, like springtime's shout.
Pizza boxes stacked, a tower of gold,
Each slice tells a story, each story retold.

Songs of the Subconscious

Singing in whispers, the thoughts that we keep,
Humming in rhythms, from dreams that we sleep.
A rubber duck choir, in vibrant attire,
Bubbles of laughter jump higher and higher.

Dancing in circles, each thought is a friend,
Twirling and spinning, no need to pretend.
Cheese mice and ghosts in a waltz on a beam,
Crafting a melody straight from a dream.

Dance of the Unknown

Under the table, where lost socks combine,
A parade of the odd, in a world so divine.
The lamp does the tango, the chair takes a bow,
While the clock chimed a hiccup, oh what an uproar now!

Shadows do shuffle, and giggles take flight,
As the curtains join in, fluttering with might.
Unseen jubilation, in corners so bright,
The dance of the strange, is pure delight!

Bridges of Contemplation

Between the odd moments, a bridge made of dream,
Carrying whispers like kids with ice cream.
Built with the laughter of echoes at play,
Skating on thoughts that just won't go away.

A stroll through the silly, where reason does flip,
Chasing the shadows that wiggle and skip.
With each step we ponder the odd and absurd,
Creating a symphony without a word.

Kaleidoscope of Vision

Colors clash, they twist and turn,
Thoughts collide, for new ideas we yearn.
A jigsaw puzzle of thoughts so bright,
In this wacky maze, ideas take flight.

A squiggly line, a polka-dotted scheme,
Dreams float around like a silly ice cream.
Laughter erupts, in this merriment dance,
Each silly thought deserves a chance!

Fires of Invention

A spark ignites, a bright little flame,
Blowing on embers, we play the game.
A toaster that dances, a clock that sings,
Who knew invention could have such wings?

A bubbling cauldron, ideas brew bold,
Mix silly potions, and watch the fun unfold.
Bubble wrap rockets, and slippers that skate,
Oh, what a world where we animate fate!

Whirlpools of Wonder

Round and round in this spiraled spree,
Twirling around with glee, oh me!
A fish wearing glasses, a cat in a hat,
In this wondrous whirlpool, imagine all that!

A rubber duck circus, it floats in the air,
Laughter erupts, without a care.
Twirling thoughts like cotton candy fluff,
In this whirlpool, there's never enough!

Breaths of Genius

Breathe in the silly, exhale the plain,
Dancing with thoughts, like drop of rain.
Jellybean dreams that twirl and bounce,
In this light-hearted world, we laugh and flounce.

Sneaky little ideas, sliding like soap,
Tickling the mind, like a joyful hope.
With each little chuckle, we dig even deep,
In this breath of genius, creativity leaps!

Landscapes of the Mind

In the fields of whimsy, ideas sprout,
Like dandelions dancing, there's no doubt.
A chicken in a tux, what a sight,
Pecking at ideas under the moonlight.

Clouds shaped like tacos, isn't it grand?
Sailing on thoughts, a carnival planned.
The sun's a big smile, the stars all wink,
As we sip on laughter, don't you think?

Mountains of giggles, valleys of cheer,
Juggling our dreams, let's give a cheer!
Banana boats sailing on oceans of glee,
In lands where silliness roams wild and free.

Paint a picture with crayons of thought,
In the corners of minds, laughter is caught.
A rollercoaster ride on a worm, what a twist,
In this playful realm, nothing's amiss!

Constellations of Thought

Stars made of marshmallows, twinkling bright,
Constellations of nonsense, pure delight.
Snafus and giggles float through the night,
As we hop from idea to silly flight.

The moon's a big cookie, baked with care,
While aliens play hopscotch in the air.
Comets of laughter zoom by so fast,
In this galaxy where fun is amassed.

Venus is winking, the sun cracks a smile,
As peanut butter planets orbit in style.
Nonsense is reigning, a joyful display,
In these starry realms, we frolic and play.

Dancing with shadows in a cosmic glow,
Jellybean meteors fall, don't you know?
Each thought is a star, shining with glee,
In the universe of humor, come fly with me!

Threads of Inspiration

Spinning tall tales on a loom made of cheese,
Where each woven thought makes everyone sneeze.
A kitten in mittens that rolls down a hill,
With a hat full of giggles and laughter to spill.

Threading through life with a needle of fun,
Where ideas bounce high like a hyperactive gun.
Puppies in pajamas dance under the sun,
In the circus of dreams, we all are the one.

Yarns of imagination twist and entwine,
As we stitch together the bizarre and divine.
A rainbow of humor arcs high in the sky,
In this fabric of nonsense, we all aim to fly.

With each crafty knot, our giggles increase,
In our world of whimsy, we find our peace.
So grab your own thread and spin it around,
In this tapestry of fun, joy knows no bound!

Echoes of the Ether

Whispers of whimsy float through the air,
With giggles and chuckles, we haven't a care.
Echoing dreams from the tips of our toes,
In this realm of laughter, who knows where it goes?

Bouncing on clouds made of cotton candy,
Puppets with voices that are quite dandy.
A concert of silliness, tune in today,
As echoes of nonsense dance and sway.

The sound of a ticklish taco truck horn,
Plays a melody bright as the early morn.
Laughter rings out from both near and far,
In this absurd world where we all are a star.

So let's raise a toast to the echoes above,
In this joyful ether, we spread our love.
With each silly sound, may our spirits take flight,
Through the echoes of laughter that fill up the night!

Galaxies of Genius in the Brain's Vault

In the vault where thoughts collide,
Ideas sprawl, oh what a ride!
Doodles dance in cosmic cheer,
While zany dreams resound so clear.

Jelly beans of colors bright,
Launch into the starry night.
With every giggle, sparks ignite,
As whimsy takes an epic flight.

Banana peels on asteroid trails,
A comet sneezes, laughter sails.
The brain's a place where quirks are gold,
Each wacky thought a tale retold.

The Tapestry of Fractured Ideas

In threads of thought, a puzzling quilt,
Each crazy stitch, a whimsy built.
A patchwork of giggles, dreams, and schemes,
Where laughter weaves through wildest beams.

Knitting rules? They're all outsmarted,
Every notion brightly charted.
A tangled web of silly plans,
Where noodle monsters dance in bands.

Stitching clouds to suit the sun,
Bursting bubbles, oh what fun!
A funky fabric, errors grand,
In this bizarre imagination land.

Chasms of Churning Visions

Deep in chasms of wacky sights,
Ideas tumble, left and right.
A whirlpool spins with glee and might,
Where goofy thoughts take joyful flight.

Outlandish creatures swirl and twirl,
As colorful chaos starts to unfurl.
Gus the giraffe skates on a star,
While alien frogs play a guitar.

In this wild, spinning abyss,
Nothing's mundane, nothing amiss.
Each twist and turn a quirky game,
In these chasms, nothing's the same.

Fissures of Fire and Fantasy

In the cracks where dreams erupt,
Fiery fancies get mixed up.
Whimsical flames flicker and dance,
As laughter joins in the crazy trance.

Marshmallow clouds, where wishes fry,
With cupcake trees touching the sky.
A dragon steals a slice of pie,
As unicorns in hats fly by.

Through the fissures, visions stream,
Frolicking in a candy dream.
Each spark a jest that winks and glows,
Where fantasy blooms and laughter grows.

Landscapes of Thought in Bloom

In a field where ideas sprout,
And giggles often break out.
Ideas swirl like bees in spring,
Bouncing high, oh what a fling!

Chasing dreams in wild disguise,
As laughter dances in the skies.
Each thought a flower, bright and bold,
Stories waiting to be told.

Puns are blooming, seeds are sown,
In this garden, joy is grown.
Whimsy tugs at curious minds,
As creativity unwinds.

So skip along this vibrant path,
Embrace the silly, break the math.
In every petal, laughter's song,
In these landscapes, we belong.

Horizons of Unbound Inspiration

Up above the clouds, we fly,
Chasing thoughts that twist and cry.
With each giggle, wings take flight,
Ideas jump like a rabbit's sight.

In the distance, colors clash,
The joy of thinking comes in a flash.
Bouncing thoughts like rubber ducks,
In this sky, we'll try our lucks.

Scribbles dance across the air,
Each word a creature full of flair.
In this realm, we'll spin and twirl,
To the rhythm of the silly whirl.

No limits here, just endless glee,
Imagination is the key.
Among the stars, our dreams we sprout,
With a chuckle and a shout.

The Pit of Endless Possibilities

In a pit where thoughts collide,
Ideas tumble like a slide.
Silly notions fall and roll,
Creating chaos, that's the goal!

A thought just slipped, where did it go?
Oh look! It's wearing quite a show.
With every laugh, more tangles spin,
In this pit, the fun begins.

Digging deep for gems of cheer,
Found a joke that makes it clear.
Endless laughter in the muck,
In this pit, we're out of luck!

So dive on in, don't be shy,
With every thought, we'll reach the sky.
Embrace the mess, let's take a leap,
In this pit, no time for sleep!

Sculpting Silhouettes of Innovation

With laughter, we carve shapes so bright,
In shadows, ideas take flight.
A silly sculptor with a grin,
Creating forms we'd never win.

Twisting clay with whimsy's grace,
Every blob a funny face.
Innovation with a twist, oh my!
Who knew a sneeze could fly so high?

Chiseling dreams from blocks of doubt,
With chortles in each playful bout.
Every stroke a chuckle shared,
In this workshop, all are spared.

So gather round, let's craft and play,
Silly forms, come what may.
In the dance of thought, let's mold and bend,
Every silhouette, a new best friend.

Intricate Designs of Thought

In a brain where ideas spin,
Thoughts pop like corn, a silly din.
One says, 'Hey, let's build a boat!'
The other replies, 'But it needs a goat!'

Sketches danced on napkin sheets,
Plans scribbled in cafes with sweets.
A blender becomes a time machine,
Don't ask how; it's all quite obscene!

Post-it notes in riotous hues,
Like confetti from creative blues.
Each peel reveals a quirky tune,
Now we've got a dancing moon!

So here's to thoughts, both wild and wacky,
Mismatched socks, oh, isn't that tacky?
Let's craft a world with giggles abound,
In this circus where ideas are crowned!

Emanations of the Spirit

Out of my head, ideas take flight,
Like a squirrel that just saw a kite.
One wiggles here, another pops out,
Like popcorn kernels in a bout!

Ideas buzz like bees in a hive,
Crafting antics that make us thrive.
A sandwich starts dancing on the plate,
While I ponder why it chose to skate!

The spirit whispers jokes in my ear,
Making mundane moments steered clear.
A taco hat, a donut scarf,
Each odd thought makes me burst with a laugh!

So let's embrace this laughter tonight,
With blunders that twirl in pure delight.
In the chaos where spirits play merry,
Life's little oddities are quite complimentary!

Fissures of Fantasy

In the land where zebras wear ties,
Unicorns prance and bake pies.
A castle built of bubblegum,
Where jellybeans play the drums!

Magic mushrooms hold court in style,
Waving their hats, they wink and smile.
One shouts, 'Let's have a tea party soon!'
With dancing chairs beneath a moon!

A dragon's breath is minty fresh,
While fairies laugh, 'Oh what a mess!'
With pizza slices floating high,
They all agree, they'll never die!

So let your dreams take a crazy chance,
Join the world in a whimsical dance.
In spills of laughter, let's find the key,
To unlock the magic that sets us free!

Pillars of Imagination

In a world built on giggles and glee,
Pillars of dreams stand tall, oh me!
One's made of marshmallows, sweet and round,
The other's a rollercoaster, upside down!

Ideas glow like bright neon lights,
A dance party beneath starry nights.
Pasta trees swaying in the breeze,
While spaghetti birds swoop down with ease!

Crafting castles from random bits,
A jumble of nonsense that truly fits.
My pet goldfish wears a little cape,
With these pillars, creativity takes shape!

So let's swing bathtubs into the sky,
And fling our worries away with a sigh.
In this realm of joy, let's play pretend,
Where imagination reigns, my dear friend!

Uncharted Territories of Art

In splashes of paint, the cat did sneak,
A masterpiece born, quite absurd, quite unique.
With spaghetti as brushes, they painted the sky,
While the dog looked confused, asking, 'Oh my?'

The canvas was sticky, a fusion of snacks,
The colors were vibrant, with some spicy flax.
A noodle for a brush, a bagel for a plate,
Creating a pizza that looked truly great.

Pies flying high like balloons in the air,
With toppings of madness, none seemed to care.
A gallery of giggles, a buffet of art,
A feast for the eyes, where nonsense would start.

Who knew that creation could taste like a dream?
In this joke of a world, we all laugh and beam.
So grab your odd tools, let your wild spirit roam,
In these playful domains, we shall all call home.

Fables of the Unwritten

Once in a land where the pencils drew dreams,
Lived a taco-loving poet, or so it seems.
His words were all tangled in cheese and in meat,
And his rhymes were all served with a side of cold feet.

He scribbled on napkins, each verse a delight,
While squirrels in bow ties danced by candlelight.
With laughter like thunder, the stories would flow,
A banquet of nonsense, come feast, don't be slow!

In this quirky fable, where llamas could sing,
The verses would tumble and thrash in a swing.
A hiccup of whimsy, a hiccup of fate,
His tales grew, much bigger, oh never too late.

Every line sprinkled with jelly and jam,
A sandwich of nonsense, as sweet as it can.
So let's add a dash of bewildering fun,
For stories unwritten are never quite done.

Twilight of Inspiration

At dusk when the crayons began to unwind,
A turtle rushed by, with his thoughts quite maligned.
He tripped over ink pots, rolled into a dream,
And splattered the sky with a giggly cream.

Stars giggled down, thinking they were the best,
While unicorns colored with zest and with jest.
In the twilight of nonsense, great tales came alive,
As pancakes debated who'd come out and thrive.

A riddle was posed by a wise old baguette,
'What's yellow and bouncy, but not quite a pet?'
The answer was laughter, with sprinkles galore,
That lived in a world where all goofy things soar.

So let's dance with shadows, as bright as a spark,
In this twilight of wonders, we'll laugh in the dark.
For imagination blooms where the twilight has grown,
A playful adventure we'll happily own.

Weavings of the Unconscious

In a web spun by dreams, a rabbit took flight,
With a hat full of giggles that dazzled the night.
He hopped upon clouds woven thick with delight,
As rainbows unraveled, oh what a sight!

With threads made of cheese, they stitched silly schemes,
And pillows of fluff where imagination beams.
The clock struck a jellybean flavor so rare,
As marshmallows floated without a single care.

There's magic in chaos, a rhythm, a rhyme,
Where nonsense dances through sugar and time.
The fabric of wishes, a quilt of pure jest,
A tapestry woven, we smile, never rest.

So let's grab our scissors, let's snip and let's sew,
In this realm of the whimsy, where laughter does grow.
For the weavings of thought are a carnival spree,
Where we patch our imaginations, wild and free.

Realms of Creation

In a land where ideas bloom,
Silly thoughts take up the room.
A chicken doodles on a page,
While cows decide to dance and engage.

The moon wears socks, oh what a sight,
And stars giggle at the quirk of night.
Rubber ducks in hats parade,
Imagination's wacky escapade!

A fish that sings a poppy tune,
In the sunshine, holding a cartoon.
Splatters of paint on biscuit trees,
All come together like sweetened peas.

Oh, here we go, a ticklish ride,
Where nonsense and laughter collide.
Giraffes juggle and pineapples race,
In this whimsical, joyful space!

Undercurrents of Fantasy

In the waves where fairies dive,
A wizard wakes just to revive.
He trips on dragons, oh dear me,
And spills his potion under a tree.

With jellybeans and unicorns,
They craft new worlds where laughter's born.
Cats wear glasses, sipping tea,
While olives dance in jubilee.

A pirate found a feathered hat,
Giggling as he strokes a cat.
He sails on a boat made of toast,
Chasing the jellyfish that boast!

In this ocean of silly dreams,
Where nothing is quite as it seems.
The laughter bubbles up like brew,
Here undercurrents paint the view!

Layers of Innovation

Beneath the roof, a monster hides,
With crayons as its playful guides.
It drawls and sketches on the floor,
Inventing things we can't ignore.

Toasters make toast while winking wide,
As monitors pull off their techie pride.
A robot grins, all shiny and bright,
Dancing like nobody's watching tonight.

Electric squirrels on roller skates,
Hurling ideas like circus crates.
One just built a castle of cheese,
While others twirl as they please.

In layers thick with goofy dreams,
Innovation's humming in zany beams.
Who knew inventing could be so fun?
With laughter echoing, we're all just one!

Waves of the Unexplored

On a tide of giggles, we float away,
Where jellyfish disco and dolphins play.
A seaweed pirate steals a glance,
While octopuses twist and dance.

Curly waves create a surprise,
As surfboards sprout wings and rise.
Bubbles of laughter, they drift and soar,
Through the ocean's vibrant door.

In this realm, a crab plays flute,
As sea turtles wear a snappy suit.
Anemones hum their melodies bright,
In waves of whimsies shining with light.

Here's to the splashes and playful sprays,
Where every tail wiggle brightens our days.
Embrace the tickles, the laughs, let it flow,
In the waves of the unexplored, we glow!

Embers of Enigma

In a world of jumbled whims,
Where socks are paired with hats,
A dancing cat in whimsies grim,
    Sings tales of flying rats.

Out of boxes, dreams take flight,
With crayons that paint the sun,
A pancake flip on a Tuesday night,
    Laughs echo till we're done.

In corners where the weirdest bloom,
A rubber chicken starts to waltz,
And every thought's a quirky room,
    Where reason takes a fault.

So here's to sparks of crazy flair,
Where giggles meet the oddest frown,
In silly games we all can share,
    Let's flip the script upside down.

Streams of Thought

A river flows with bubbles bright,
Where fish can sing and frogs can dance,
And every drop shines pure delight,
While chickens hold a merry prance.

Upstream, the ducks wear tiny hats,
Hatching plans to steal some bread,
As squirrels join in with acrobat chats,
And tumble down to spread their spread.

The sunbeams tickle the water's face,
As giggles swirl with every wave,
In this odd little, happy place,
A creativity we crave.

So grab your friends and paddle near,
In currents wild and filled with jest,
A journey bursting with good cheer,
Where nonsense always beats the best.

Veins of the Vibrant

Through vibrant lands where colors clash,
A purple cow begins to skate,
While polka-dots make quite the splash,
Dancing in a wobbly state.

On every tree, a jester sways,
With bubblegum and silly hats,
They laugh and sing for hours and days,
While drawing mustached cats.

In gardens where the giggles grow,
A rainbow twists into a slide,
The flowers cheer, "Come join the show!"
As dreams take off on a wild ride.

So let your heart be light and free,
With each bizarre and vivid scheme,
In hues of joy and harmony,
We'll paint the world—a funny dream.

Lighthouses of Creativity

On rocky shores with neon lights,
A lighthouse stands with jelly beans,
It wobbles in the wondrous nights,
Guiding ships made out of dreams.

With beams of joy that bounce and twirl,
Dancers leap from rock to sand,
And every thought begins to swirl,
As giggles paint the land so grand.

From every window, funny sights,
With penguins wearing winter hats,
They wave and hum in dancing flights,
While jokes fly like acrobats.

So find your light—let shadows fade,
In laughter's glow, we boldly play,
Our quirky paths will never jade,
For in this fun, we'll always stay.

Caverns of Creation

In the depths of my favorite hat,
A jolly raccoon chats with a cat.
They plot wild schemes on a cheese flat,
While dancing around with a fishy spat.

Crayons scattered across the floor,
They doodle dreams; oh, what a score!
A giraffe in boots needs to explore,
Singing nonsense—who could ask for more?

Bubbles bounce with giggles galore,
An octopus plays a wild floor score.
It juggles ink and metaphor,
While scribbles grow to legend lore.

In my mind, puddles of paint,
A world where worries begin to faint.
Surreal tales with a hint of quaint,
Where laughter reigns, a joyful saint.

Ripples of Potential

A penguin in a polka dot suit,
Waltzes with chickens—what a hoot!
They bake a cake with extra glute,
And fight a crab with a shiny boot.

Marshmallow clouds float in the sky,
Swirling around like a giant pie.
They're tossing sprinkles, oh my, oh my!
While unicorns serve drinks with a sigh.

Octagonal bubbles of giggly fun,
Bounce over hills, each a shining sun.
The rules of gravity? They've sadly run,
As puns fly high, all the world's won.

A parasol spins with laughter inside,
While snail races paint landscapes wide.
In this realm where whimsy can't hide,
Silly adventures take us for a ride.

Sparks in Silence

In a library, whispering cats,
Read novels on giant mats.
They chase phantoms with hats and bats,
While pondering why socks go in spats.

A frying pan sings a tune so sweet,
As muffins dance on little feet.
They plot to hold a grand elite,
A breakfast ball to which all meet.

Glitter fairies twirl and spin,
Painting dreams with a cheeky grin.
With a wink they let the magic in,
Sprouting giggles that never thin.

In corners where hiccups reign supreme,
Llamas sip tea and plot a meme.
Creativity flows like a bubbling stream,
Where every thought is a spark, it would seem.

Mosaic of the Mind's Eye

With jellybeans forming a road,
A rubber chicken wears a code.
It clucks a symphony, bold and strode,
While marshmallow clouds lower the load.

Gnomes in pajamas knit nightlight stars,
While sipping lemonade from broken jars.
Twirling around in a dance with cars,
Riding the moon on rubber guitars.

Disco squirrels with shiny tails,
Celebrate victory, sipping ales.
While the wind whispers glorious tales,
Of sandwiches sailing with thin veils.

In a world where nonsense takes the lead,
Creativity's a quirky breed.
Painting laughter in colors freed,
Where the rhythm of joy is the heart's creed.

The Abyss of Boundless Creativity

In a world where ideas just play,
Noodles and thoughts swirl each day.
Silly schemes bounce like a ball,
Dreams of penguins wearing a shawl.

Colors of nonsense dance in the sun,
Doodle monsters just having fun.
When crayons argue, who fills the page?
It's a circus act on a bright stage.

Ideas leap like frogs on a log,
While penguins wiggle and dance like a cog.
The toast talks back to the buttered jam,
Oh look, there's a chicken in a frying pan!

And when you fall into this delight,
You'll giggle and grin with pure delight.
For the abyss is bright and the sketches are bold,
A treasure chest of wonders to behold.

Springs of Surreal Sentiment

Gummy bears float above the trees,
Wishing for ice cream with a side of peas.
A river flows with fizzy drinks,
While marshmallows dance before you blink.

Kites made of socks soar through the blue,
Each twist and turn brings laughter anew.
Salad dressed in polka-dot sauce,
Makes the lunchtime chaos a playful gloss.

The clouds wear hats, all bright and funny,
As bees recite poetry sweet as honey.
And if you slip on a banana peel,
Remember, it's part of the grand surreal!

A dreamscape where giggles never cease,
And every mishap is a joyful piece.
So dive into springs that gush with cheer,
Where whimsy and laughter make life dear.

Echoing Valleys of Vision

Echoing laughter fills the air,
As squirrels debate their next grand affair.
Chickens in tuxedos strut with pride,
In valleys where imaginations collide.

Upside-down rainbows brighten the sky,
While turtles sing ballads to passersby.
The mountains giggle with each silly shout,
As thoughts bounce around like a rubber ball route.

In the valleys where nonsense reigns true,
Balloons play chess with a wise kangaroo.
Prancing polka dots dance with flair,
And echoing chuckles are everywhere!

So join the mirth in this happy scene,
Where every thought is a playful glean.
In the echoing valleys, let's take flight,
For envisioning joy is pure delight!

The Labyrinth of Luminary Ideas

In the maze of thoughts, what do we find?
A banana rocket ship, oh so kind!
With walls of cereal and ceilings of toast,
A journey of whimsy, let's raise a toast!

Pizza capes twirl in cosmic tracks,
As giggling ghosts carry snacks on their backs.
Each twist and turn brings a brand-new jest,
Even the shadows are wearing a vest!

Tickles and chuckles meander through halls,
With cupcake staircases, no one stalls.
The riddle of laughter lingers and sways,
In the labyrinth where frolic forever plays.

So wander these paths without any fear,
For the maze is alive with joy and cheer.
Let ideas stumble, juggle, and trip,
In this whimsical world, let your dreams skip!

Pockets of Potential Unfolding

In pockets deep where giggles hide,
Laughter bubbles, our minds collide.
Like jellybeans tossed in a fray,
Ideas get silly, come out to play.

Beneath the couch, a treasure trove,
Sticky notes dance and clever jokes rove.
A banana peel here, a meme over there,
Creative chaos fills the air.

With crayons and glue, we craft delight,
Turning boredom into a circus of light.
Each doodle a spark, each scribble a scream,
In this playful land, we dare to dream.

So gather your thoughts, let's mix them well,
In pockets of fun, there's magic to sell.
We'll paint the walls with our wildest tales,
In laughter and joy, our spirit prevails.

The Basin of Uncharted Ideas

In a basin deep where notions gather,
Wonders float by, and we all just tather.
With wild hats and socks that don't match,
We launch ideas, like a creative batch.

A rubber duck sails through waves of thought,
Every splish and splash, a new scheme caught.
With a wink and a grin, we twist and we bend,
Finding shapes in the water where imaginations blend.

Want to make spaghetti from rain in the sky?
In this basin of dreams, we give it a try.
With noodle balloons and choux pastry stars,
We craft our own world, no matter how bizarre.

So come, dip your toes in the whirlpool's joke,
Let's muddle through thoughts until we all choke,
In this silly stream, where ideas are free,
We'll swim in the laughter, just you and me.

Wellsprings of Wonder and Whimsy

At wells where giggles bubble and flow,
Springs of whimsy, watch ideas grow.
From teacups to toasters, we dream up a feast,
A noodle that dances, our laughter increased.

As we splash in the puddles of winks and sighs,
The well is a fountain where creativity flies.
Old socks become puppets with stories galore,
And every odd thought opens yet another door.

Come sip from the joy where nonsense is king,
Each drop is a smile, a curious thing.
In this well of delight, we frolic and twirl,
With each giggle we find, a new thought unfurls.

So raise up your cup, my whimsical friend,
Let's chuckle and cheer, there's no need to pretend.
For in these wild springs, where laughter's the key,
We'll splash in pure joy, just you and me.

Fractal Dreams in the Mind's Terrain

In the mind's maze, thoughts twist and twine,
Fractal dreams giggle, they shimmer and shine.
Like a jigsaw puzzle with pieces askew,
We fit in the fun, with plenty to do.

Who knew that a thought could grow so bizarre?
A broccoli rocket, or a dancing guitar.
From unicorns baking cakes made of lace,
In this crinkled realm, there's magic to embrace.

Ideas spin out, like glittery threads,
Connecting our dreams as we lie in our beds.
Each nook a new vision, each cranny a tale,
With laughter as fuel, we set our minds sail.

So cherish the odd, the silly and strange,
In this fractal landscape, we love to arrange.
For here in our minds, where the wild things dart,
Life is a gallery of wonder and art.

Reflections in the Canvas

A smudge of paint, a brush that's shy,
My masterpiece is a sneaky pie.
With polka dots and zigzag flair,
It's a wonder if it's art or air.

The colors dance, they leap and twirl,
The canvas giggles, a playful swirl.
Splatters flying, oh what a sight,
My paint has taken a daring flight!

A cat with stripes, a dog in shoes,
Why not? Art's meant to amuse!
I'll hang it high, let feedback roll,
Just hope it doesn't eat my soul!

So here's to chaos, art that's bold,
My funny canvas, a sight to behold!
Every stroke, a comical tale,
In the land where creativity sets sail.

Spirals of Thought

Round and round my mind does race,
Thoughts like spirals begin to chase.
A light bulb flickers, then it dims,
I wonder where the logic swims?

I ponder sandwiches and the sky,
Why does toast always like to fly?
A noodle's dance, a burger's whine,
In this tangle, I seek the divine.

Flip a coin, let fortune play,
Should I dance or sit all day?
Ideas tumble, a merry mess,
With witty banter, I must confess.

So here within this spiral spree,
Creativity's laughing with glee.
I'll catch a thought, I'll twist and shout,
In this carnival, I'll twist about.

Horizons of the Mind

On the horizon, ideas sprout,
Bouncing wildly, round about.
A cloud of giggles drifts and sways,
Where do they go on windy days?

In fields of stars and silly dreams,
Unicorns dance in moonlit beams.
I chase a thought on roller skates,
Love how it wobbles, it elevates!

The sun is laughing, the sky a grin,
With every thought, I dive right in.
Pies in the sky, a jellybean sea,
My mind finds joy in absurdity.

So let's ride waves of imagination,
Sailing high on the laughter nation.
Each horizon, a laugh to unwind,
In this funny maze, I'll surely find.

Fragments of the Unseen

I gather pieces, odd and rare,
From jellybeans to thinning air.
A broken clock, a crooked shoe,
What do they make? A vibrant view!

In shadows flicker colors bright,
The unseen laughs, a playful sight.
A whisper here, a giggle there,
The fragments swirl without a care.

An octopus wearing a chef's hat,
Cooking pasta with a sturdy cat.
Why not create such joy today?
In the land where silly thoughts play.

With every shard, a tale unfolds,
In the wacky, the brave, the bold.
Embrace the madness, seek the cheer,
In unseen fragments, fun is near.

The Gaps Between Thoughts Unclear.

In the middle of a gray old day,
Thoughts just take a runaway foray.
I start to think of pies and cakes,
Forget the reason, oh, what a mistake!

Ideas dance like leaves in the breeze,
Each one giggles—"Hey! Look at me, please!"
But when I reach out, they all disappear,
Leaving me with just thoughts full of cheer!

I scribble notes, all a jumbled mess,
'Buy more candy!'—my favorite stress.
And when I wonder where my mind went,
It's likely deep into the pudding tent!

So when I think, let the laughter flow,
For every blank space, there's room for a show.
Gaps in my brain can be filled with delight,
Where nonsense can flourish, oh what a sight!

Echoes in the Abyss

In a void where thoughts seem to play,
Echoes giggle, making my mind sway.
"Did you remember to feed the cat?"
No, I was busy imagining a hat!

Whispers bounce like rubber balls high,
Questions like squirrels zip by, oh my!
I chase them down with a giggle and grin,
But they slip away—such a mischievous kin!

Ghosts of ideas float in the dark,
Making me ponder and miss my mark.
'What was I saying?' I scratch my head,
Oh well, here's another thought instead!

In the abyss where my brain likes to roam,
Echoes of laughter find their way home.
So join the chaos of my whimsical spree,
Together we'll dance like the wildest of bees!

Whispers of Inspiration

A whisper floats in the air so light,
It tickles my ears, oh what a delight!
What was the thought? I'm sure it was grand,
But now it's a wisp, just slipping like sand.

I chase the muse with a cupcake in hand,
"Inspiration, stay!" I demand and demand.
Yet she giggles and bounces just out of reach,
Leaving me with crumbs for my brain to teach!

Ideas tend to play peek-a-boo,
Bandits of logic, just who are you?
In the realm of thoughts, I wander and dance,
Finding new joys in a creative trance!

So I laugh at the game, quite silly indeed,
For whispers of brilliance are just what I need.
When inspiration plays with my mind in a whirl,
It's a mad little secret, my colorful pearl!

Pockets of Imagination

Deep in my pockets, ideas do hide,
Lizards and unicorns all side by side.
A treasure of wonders, a jumbled cache,
Oh look, there's a cloud with a colorful sash!

I pull out a whim, a sprinkle of zest,
Mix laughter with nonsense, it's all for the best.
Chasing the dragon that lives in my sock,
It whispers sweet secrets, oh what a shock!

In the garden of nonsense where all thoughts bloom,
I find my solutions amidst the loud boom.
With giggles and chuckles, my ideas take flight,
In pockets of magic, I welcome the night!

So stash your own treasures, don't let them decay,
For imagination's spark lights up the dull day.
In each pocket of whimsy, let laughter unfurl,
Join me in giggles, let's dance in a swirl!

Shadows of the Muse

In a dark corner, ideas hide,
Like socks lost in the laundry tide,
They poke out their heads, then they leap,
As I chase them, I tumble and weep.

A beret-wearing cat plays the fool,
Juggling thoughts like they're old-school,
With a whisk of his tail, he sends them flying,
While I'm left here giggling and crying.

A sandwich smeared with peanut butter,
Inspiration's odd frothy utter,
I take a bite, and out pops a pun,
Who knew lunch could be so much fun?

Lost in a maze of my own delight,
Where even the shadows giggle at night,
With a wink and a nod, they lead me on,
Creating a world where laughter is drawn.

Landscapes of Innovation

A hill made of post-it notes unfolds,
Where every color tells tales untold,
I paint with ideas, splashes of bright,
While my coffee pot bubbles, ready to fight.

An office chair spins like a merry-go-round,
Ideas thrown like confetti, colorful and round,
I trip over dreams as I spin with glee,
In this vibrant world, I'm a wild jubilee.

Sketches come alive, dancing on the wall,
They whisper of madness, and I heed their call,
With a cat in a hat, we draft up a scheme,
For a new kind of ride, or perhaps, just a meme.

Riding on puns, we gather the crew,
Building castles of laughter—who knew?
When creativity strikes, we all take a bow,
In these lands of invention, let's party right now!

Depths of Dreamscapes

In a world where clouds wear silly hats,
And birds discuss politics with chitchat,
I dive into dreams like a synchronized swim,
Where each splash of joy is never too grim.

A river of chocolate flows downhill,
Where marshmallow boats glide, giving a thrill,
I snack on the shore, while ideas take flight,
Turning whispers to giggles under the moonlight.

Giant pencils scribble on the grass,
Drawing plans for a waltz with the sass,
I twirl through the pages, a dance of delight,
In a realm where imagination takes flight.

The sun waves its rays like a playful tease,
Painting everything golden with breezy ease,
As laughter echoes in these dreamscapes so bright,
I drift through the wonder, my heart light as kite.

Patterns in the Void

In nothingness, I found a dance,
A waltz of ideas, a detailed glance,
Shapes swirl and twirl like a dizzy parade,
With laughter and joy, my fears quickly fade.

An empty canvas can't hold me back,
Each blank space is a treasure, not a lack,
I doodle a dragon that hisses with glee,
Where the void becomes a party of three.

Music from nowhere fills the air,
As shadows clap with whimsical flair,
Patterns emerge from the giggles we weave,
Crafting a puzzle no one can believe.

With a wink at the stars, we dance through the night,
Finding patterns in nothing, pure delight,
So here's to the chaos, the fun we deploy,
In the land of the void, we all share the joy.

The Oasis of Originality

In a desert of dull ideas, a mirage we see,
A splash of weird thoughts, like a wild cup of tea.
A cactus in a top hat, dancing with glee,
Twirling in circles, shouting, "Look at me!"

Sand dunes are giggling, they tickle our feet,
As we sip on the nectar, oh what a treat!
Bright colors explode, like a candy shop's beat,
Jellybeans rain down, such a whimsical feat!

Be daring, be silly; embrace all your quirks,
In this oasis, we're all just big jerks.
With laughter as fuel, we'll conquer our works,
Every mishap a rhyme, and joy never shirks!

So let's ride a mirage on waves of sweet glee,
Where the bunnies are kings and the fish dance like bees.
In this funny land, we're all meant to be,
Creators of joy, you and I, don't you see?

Valleys of Visionary Vortex

In a valley of giggles, the vortex spins round,
Ideas take flight, on a trampoline bound.
A whirl of odd visions, like a lost circus clown,
The logic escapes us — it's nowhere to be found!

Silly hats cascade, in colors so bright,
As we leap through the air, chasing dreams in the night.
Chickens in tuxedos, a bizarre, joyful sight,
They dance in the moonlight, oh what pure delight!

The vortex is buzzing, it whirls up our frowns,
Creating confetti from whimsical towns.
With laughter as currency, we'll wear silly crowns,
And skateboard on rainbows, no need for bounds!

So join in the fun, let's spin with the breeze,
Wear your quirkiest shoes, and climb up the trees.
In these valleys of laughter, we do as we please,
As the world spins around us, it's all just a tease!

Seeds of Change in Fertile Minds

In gardens of laughter, where oddities grow,
We plant little seeds, and they put on a show.
A potato in glasses, a carrot in tow,
They dance at the moonlight, bringing joy in a flow.

Twirling and spinning, ideas start sprout,
Dancing with mushrooms, they turn life about.
With every odd notion, we cheer and we shout,
In this field of the quirky, we deeply root out!

Peppers in capes fly—a superhero crew,
Lettuce debating what fruit's, veggie too!
In this garden of whimsy, our laughter is true,
Creating a world where imagination grew!

So sprinkle the soil with your thoughts that surprise,
Watch the laughter blossom and shine in the skies.
Every idea a flower; let's open our eyes,
In fertile minds, we find joy that never dies!

Ripples in the Sea of Thought

In a sea of ideas, waves crash with delight,
A fish in a tuxedo swims by with a kite.
Sandcastles glisten, under stars shining bright,
While jellybeans waltz in this magical night.

Ripples of laughter make circles on sand,
With octopuses juggling, oh isn't it grand?
A surfboard of silliness, ready to ride,
As we splash through the waters, with joy as our guide!

Seashells are whispering secrets of mirth,
As dolphins play pranks, giving joy a rebirth.
In this ocean of whimsy, we find our worth,
With every silly ripple, we dance and we girth!

So dive in the waves, let your worries be light,
Where the world swirls with nonsense, wrapping us tight.

In this sea full of wonders, our dreams take flight,
With laughter as our compass, we'll soar through the night!

Phenomena of Expression

In the bathroom, the best ideas bloom,
While I craft lyrics with soap in the room.
The mirror reflects a genius at play,
Singing my heart out, come night or day.

My dog, he joins in, barking a tune,
Under the glow of the neon moon.
He's a born star with a tail that twirls,
Together we conquer the galaxy of swirls.

Grab a spatula, flip that pancake style,
We'll make a feast that's worth the while.
One bite and the kitchen's a creative mess,
But what's a little flour? It's pure happiness!

As we dance with the dust, let laughter flow,
For every mishap is a chance for a show.
Spagetthis with ketchup—voilà, a delight,
In this whimsical world, we take flight!

Mixing popcorn with jelly? Why not dare!
In the realm of oddity, we've no need to care.
With smiles like sunshine and giggles that spread,
We're the architects of nonsense, color our bread!

Serendipity in Silence

In quiet corners, ideas collide,
Balloons filled with laughter begin to glide.
Whispers of wonders float through the air,
Sipping my tea, I'm a jovial bear.

Overhearing a cat narrate my dreams,
Scribbling down words that flow like streams.
In the land of the awkward, we stumble and trip,
Falling on giggles, let's take a dip!

The cake that I made got a life of its own,
It bounced on the table, and I'm not alone.
"What's the flavor?" it asked, with frosting so bright,
"Chocolate, or maybe coconut, what's your bite?"

Exploring my thoughts like a ship lost at sea,
Navigating riddles made mostly of glee.
With a side of a pickle and joy all around,
We'll feast on odd pairings, delightfully bound!

A sneeze sets off laughter like dominoes fall,
The moments we cherish are funny and small.
In the stillness of silence, the giggles erupt,
Creating a symphony, joyously corrupt!

Celestial Sparks

Stars twinkle above in an artistic display,
While I juggle my thoughts that flutter and sway.
Balloons filled with ink burst in midair,
As crayons tap dance, painting dreams everywhere.

Each comet that zooms is a joke in disguise,
Whipping up laughter that twinkles in eyes.
In the chaos of stardust, I'm throwing a fit,
Crafting a universe that's perfectly split.

With marshmallows flying like clouds in a race,
S'mores hug the moon, oh what a sweet place!
Building a rocket from spoons and some glue,
And taking off boldly with laughter as fuel.

Popcorn falls softly like tiny white stars,
Zipping through galaxies in sugar-filled jars.
Every giggle is fuel for the journey we make,
With a dash of absurdity, no chance for a break!

Slipping on dreams like they're freshly mopped floors,
We trip into laughter, and out through the doors.
In the vastness of fun, we'll never fall through,
Painting the cosmos with joy—who knew?

Elysium of Ideas

In a garden of giggles, concepts run free,
With broccoli trees that chat to the bee.
They're plotting a party under cherry balloons,
Where donuts wear dresses and dance to the tunes.

Clouds made of cupcakes float high in the skies,
While rain showers sprinkles that glitter and rise.
Lollipops grow in a technicolor hue,
As clouds laugh so loudly they're turning bright blue!

Whimsical wonders, emotions take flight,
With voice-activated toasters that sing every night.
They pop out warm bread with a wink and a grin,
"Hey, butter me up, let's begin this din!"

Every splash of creative adds color to day,
As unicorns prance in a merry ballet.
With socks on my hands, I may look quite absurd,
Yet in this wild dance, my joy can't be curbed!

So come join the laughter, the madness, the flair,
In this paradise of thoughts, there's fun everywhere.
With whimsical dreams, we compose and we play,
Creating a symphony, the silly way!

Threads of the Abyss

In a world where ideas play,
Threads hang loose in a bright display.
Tangled, twisted, a splendid mess,
We laugh out loud, no need to stress.

Bright colors clash, a bizarre delight,
In every swirl, there's a whimsical sight.
Creativity spills, like paint from a can,
Who needs a plan? Just be a fan!

Fuzzy squirrels dance on the page,
Chasing rainbows, setting the stage.
With each leap, they weave their own show,
In threads of nonsense, we jovially flow.

So join the fun, let your thoughts fly,
Embrace the chaos, give it a try.
In this abyss where laughter reigns,
We'll stitch our dreams, ignore the pains.

Imprints of Uncertainty

Footprints in a garden of doubt,
Squishy thoughts roam about.
One's a rabbit, one's a shoe,
What do they mean? A riddle for you!

Each step leaves behind a quirk,
Where will they lead? We just smirk.
A dance of oddities, joy unconfined,
The map's a scribble, but isn't it fine?

Here we stumble, there we fly,
With giggles loud enough to touch the sky.
Should we listen to wise old owls?
Or follow the path of singing scowls?

Imprints of chaos, a zany parade,
In a whimsical world, we won't be swayed.
So tiptoe or leap, come join the spree,
In happy uncertainty, we're wild and free!

Ascents of the Imagination

Up the hill of wacky schemes,
We frolic and tumble in silly themes.
With roller coaster thoughts in tow,
We laugh out loud, and off we go!

Each peak is a giggle, a funny surprise,
Where lollipops grow and candy flies.
Clouds of marshmallow fluff puff away,
In our ascent, we dance and sway.

Spin like tops, twirl so bright,
In the land of dreams, we feel just right.
Fueled by whimsy, no weight to bear,
We float on hopes, light as air.

With every climb, more joy we find,
Tickling our hearts, and free our mind.
So let's fulfill our wildest wish,
In the heights of laughter, let's thrive and swish!

Nebulas of the Mind

In the cosmos of thoughts, colors collide,
Where giggles and snickers play side by side.
The stars are made of jellybean bright,
In a nebula of nonsense, we soar with delight.

Cosmic jokes and puns twirl around,
Like wild comets that never touch ground.
Funny little aliens with hats askew,
What's the punchline? It's up to you!

Wisps of dreams float here and there,
Swirling together in a playful air.
Laughter bursts in playful bursts,
In this cosmic chaos, we quench our thirst.

So grab a star, give it a whirl,
In nebulas of the mind, watch ideas unfurl.
With every giggle, we create and bind,
In this universe, we're joyfully blind.

Touching the Void of Inspiration

A pencil's lost, it rolls away,
Chasing doodles, come what may.
The paper sighs, it bends and creaks,
As ideas play hide and seek.

The coffee's cold, my brain's on strike,
I question if I'm smart or like,
A squirrel on caffeine, hopping 'round,
In search of thoughts that can astound.

The page simply mocks, a blank-faced grin,
Where are the gems of wit I spin?
A cat walks by, sits on my muse,
Now I'm left with squirrel and blues.

A dance of words, a circus show,
My chair's a throne in this sideshow.
I'll take a bow, the crowd's aghast,
"Who knew inspiration could be such a blast?"

The Pocket of Infinite Dreams

In pockets deep, where dreams reside,
I found a sock with tales inside.
Adventures lost in laundry's lock,
Where mismatched mates swim 'round the clock.

The toaster's a portal, or so they say,
To worlds of crumbs and toasty prey.
A spatula waves, "Join the fun!"
Amidst the drips of jam, I run.

The fridge has secrets, food lost in grime,
Whispers of dinners past in cosmic rhyme.
Dancing pickles, serenading cheese,
Yet the leftovers just don't please.

Within my pocket, magic flows,
A thumb war with future, where anything goes.
A giggle hides in a jelly jar,
Tomorrow's dreams reach out so far.

Sparks from the Depths

From the depths of my cluttered mind,
Emerge strange musings, one of a kind.
A rubber duck on a pirate spree,
Plunders thoughts, just wait and see.

With grease and giggles, I craft my tales,
Of snail mail warriors with wind in their sails.
The laughter erupts, it catches fire,
Creating mischief, lifting higher.

A circus of thoughts, they twirl and spin,
Inventive chaos, that's where I win.
The paperclips dance, the ink's too thick,
In the humorous depths, I'm feeling slick.

Let's turn this jigsaw of nonsense bright,
With sparkles and giggles into the night.
Digging deep where the fun ignites,
A treasure of whimsy in playful flights.

Ascents into Boundless Imagination

I climb the hills of thought anew,
Where rubberbands launch ideas askew.
The clouds are taffy, so soft and sweet,
While gummy bears dance on my feet.

Up here the whispers of visions bloom,
Like cheese in a fondue pot of doom.
A giggle erupts, it takes to the skies,
And piñatas burst with candy surprise.

I leap from peak to peak with zest,
Trying to find the jester's nest.
Each thought a trampoline springs delight,
Bouncing around in the frothy light.

With kites of color, my dreams take wing,
And laughter echoes in the joy we bring.
In this world, where nonsense reigns,
Imagination flows like happy grains.

Echoing Dreams

In my head, ideas tumble and fall,
Like socks misplaced at the laundry ball.
Moonbeams dance on my silly schemes,
Chasing giggles in half-formed dreams.

Laughter bounces off my brain's walls,
A wild party where nonsense calls.
Imagination sprinkles confetti bright,
Juggling thoughts like a clown at night.

Each whimsy whispers a secret cheer,
While polka-dots spin in endless gear.
Bananas talking in quirky tones,
Creating a ruckus in my funny bones.

Witty sketches on a tinfoil stage,
Cackling characters leave me amazed.
In my mind's circus, chaos is king,
Where even the rubber chicken can sing.

Footprints in the Ether

A cloud of giggles trails behind,
As my thoughts race, trying to unwind.
Footprints left in a whimsical haze,
Like a cat dancing in a daze.

Bubblegum dreams stick to my shoe,
For every notion, there's something new.
Candy wrappers map my bizarre stroll,
Like confetti for every wild goal.

Lollipop lovers in woolen suits,
Tap dance to melodies from radish flutes.
Pies in the sky, and marshmallow trees,
Creating a canvas that inspires glee.

With every step, the laughter flows,
In the chirping of unbaked dough bows.
Puddle jumping in a world so bright,
Where giggles bubble under starlight.

Chronicles of the Mind

In the library of silly thoughts,
Bookshelves burst with chocolate knots.
Each chapter a kangaroo in flight,
Flipping through pages, what a sight!

Giggles scribble across the spines,
Whimsical poems in crayon lines.
The stories are wild, the plots absurd,
Talking goldfish play hopscotch unheard.

A court of jesters, a crown of cheese,
Debating the merits of ticklish bees.
Every laughter corner has its own song,
In this odd journey where I belong.

Stories weave like spaghetti skies,
Where spaghetti monsters play hide-and-seek pies.
A memoir of laughter, a tale of delight,
My mind's favorite playground, oh what a sight!

Tapestry of Ideas

Threads of color swirl and spin,
Weaving hilarity hidden within.
A patchwork of smiles, and quirks galore,
Each knot a giggle, each stitch a roar.

Rainbow balloons float through the air,
Tickling thoughts without a care.
A yo-yo rhythm in a wind-up race,
Juggling ideas with a silly face.

Mismatched socks on a tangled line,
Doing the cha-cha, feeling just fine.
Ideas whirl like a hula hoop,
In this merry, chaotic loop.

A tapestry woven with threads of jest,
In the fabric of fun, I feel the best.
With every twist, a giggle released,
In my world of laughter, I'm forever pleased.

www.ingramcontent.com/pod-product-compliance
Lightning Source LLC
Chambersburg PA
CBHW051648160426
43209CB00004B/836